Termites

ABDO
Publishing Company

Big Buddy BOOKS
Insects

Julie Murray

VISIT US AT
www.abdopublishing.com

Published by ABDO Publishing Company, 8000 West 78th Street, Edina, Minnesota 55439.

Copyright © 2011 by Abdo Consulting Group, Inc. International copyrights reserved in all countries. No part of this book may be reproduced in any form without written permission from the publisher. Big Buddy Books™ is a trademark and logo of ABDO Publishing Company.

Printed in the United States of America, North Mankato, Minnesota.
042010
092010

 PRINTED ON RECYCLED PAPER

Coordinating Series Editor: Rochelle Baltzer
Editor: Sarah Tieck
Contributing Editors: Heidi M.D. Elston, Megan M. Gunderson, BreAnn Rumsch, Marcia Zappa
Graphic Design: Maria Hosley
Cover Photograph: *Minden Pictures*: Piotr Naskrecki.
Interior Photographs/Illustrations: *iStockphoto*: ©iStockphoto.com/grecosvet (p. 14), ©iStockphoto.com/WebSubstance (pp. 5, 19); *Minden Pictures*: Thomas Marent (pp. 5, 23), Piotr Naskrecki (p. 11), Kim Taylor/npl (pp. 29), Christian Ziegler (p. 21); *Peter Arnold, Inc.*: ©Biosphoto/Gilson François (p. 7), Martin Harvey (p. 15), WILDLIFE (p. 25); *Photo Researchers, Inc.*: Anthony Bannister (pp. 5, 24), Gregory G. Dimijian, M.D. (p. 17), Pascal Goetgheluck (p. 26), Robert and Jean Pollock (p. 9), Norm Thomas (p. 13); *Shutterstock*: Melinda Fawver (pp. 5, 30), Michael Pettigrew (p. 22), Photobank (p. 15), Dr. Morley Read (pp. 5, 30), BONNIE WATTON (p. 27).

Library of Congress Cataloging-in-Publication Data

Murray, Julie, 1969-
  Termites / Julie Murray.
    p. cm. -- (Insects)
  ISBN 978-1-61613-488-4
  1. Termites--Juvenile literature. I. Title. II. Series: Murray, Julie, 1969- Insects.
  QL529.M87 2010
  595.7'36--dc22
                            2010000789

Contents

Insect World

Millions of insects live throughout the world. They are found on the ground, in the air, and in the water. Some have existed since before there were dinosaurs!

Termites are one type of insect. Termites live in large groups called colonies. They are found in many different places, including forests and deserts. They especially like warm, wet places such as jungles.

Bug Bite!

Termites are most closely related to cockroaches.

There are more than 2,000 different types of termites!

A Termite's Body

Like all insects, a termite has three main body parts. These are the head, the **thorax**, and the **abdomen**.

A termite's head has two antennae and a mouth. Termites use their antennae to smell and to find food. **Jaws** are part of a termite's mouth. Some termites have large, strong jaws for fighting. Many have smaller jaws for chewing.

Bug Bite!

Most termites do not have eyes. It is dark in their nests, so they don't need to see.

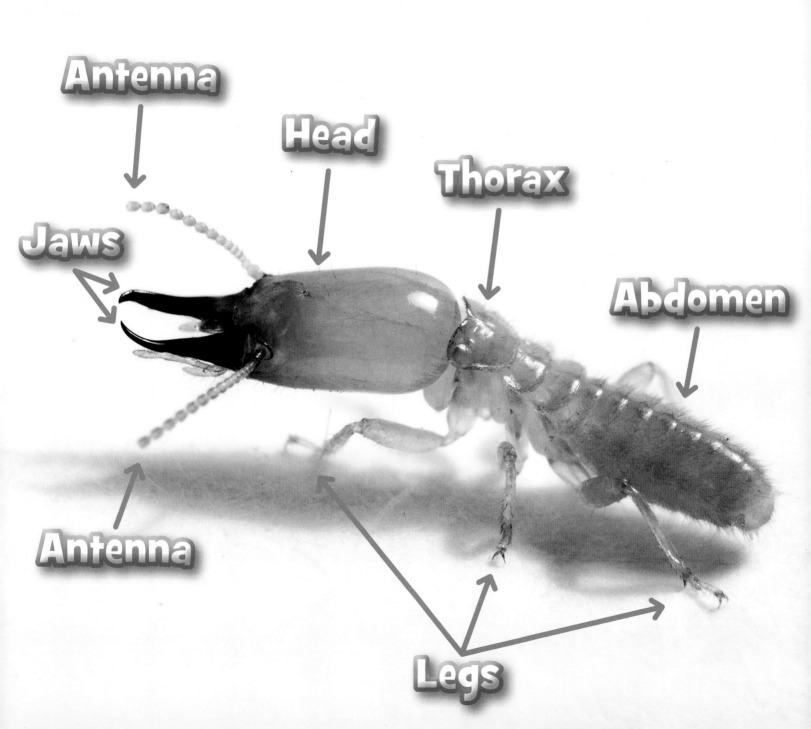

Termites have six legs connected to the **thorax**. They use them to get from place to place. Their legs can also sense movement.

A termite's thorax has room for four wings. Only termites that leave the colony to **mate** grow wings. These termites are called alates (AY-layts). Later, their wings fall off.

A termite's **abdomen** holds important **organs**. Queen termites hold eggs inside the abdomen.

Alates have wings and eyes. These features help them fly away to mate.

Life Cycle

A termite goes through three life stages. These stages are egg, nymph (NIHMF), and adult.

Like other insects, all termites begin life as eggs. After the colony's queen and king **mate**, the queen lays eggs. In a new colony, the queen and king care for the eggs. Other termites do this job after the colony grows.

Bug Bite!

Some types of termite queens can lay thousands of eggs every day!

Life Cycle of a Termite

Egg

Nymph

Adult

In time, termite nymphs **hatch** from the eggs. Nymphs have pale skin when they are born.

As the nymphs eat, their bodies become too big for their skin. So, they **shed** many times. This is called molting. After molting, nymphs become adults. Some termites molt again after becoming adults.

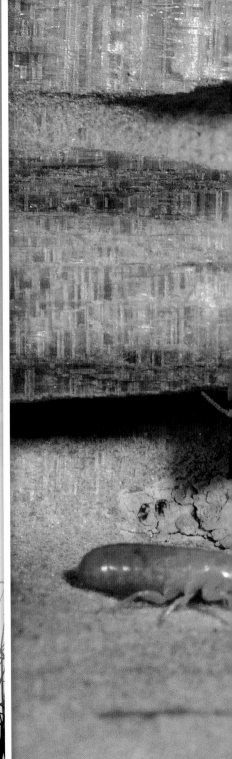

Some nymphs help care for their colonies. They build nests and care for younger nymphs.

Smart Builders

Termite colonies live in nests. Their nests are well constructed. They are made from mud and termite spit.

Some termites build nests in the wood they eat. Many dig nests underground. Others build mounds to live in.

Some termites build nests on trees or poles.

A termite mound is constructed to help the colony stay healthy and safe. It has a system of tunnels that move air. And, it has rooms above and below the ground.

Bug Bite!

The tallest termite mound was found in Africa. It was 42 feet (13 m) high!

Queen and King

A colony begins with two reproductives. These are the queen and the king. Together, they make a small nest and **mate**. Their young become workers or soldiers.

Over time, the colony grows. After a while, some of the young become alates. They leave the nest to start new colonies.

Some types of termites have extra reproductives that help with egg laying. They may take over if anything happens to the king or the queen.

A queen's abdomen swells with eggs. To protect her eggs, the queen usually lives deep within the nest. That way, it's harder for predators to find her.

Workers and Soldiers

Most termites in a colony are workers. They build and care for the nest. Some leave the nest to find wood or other food.

Workers feed the queen and the king and care for their young. They also feed and clean the soldiers.

Soldiers guard their colony's nest. They **protect** it from invaders, such as ants.

A termite nest may be an active home for more than 70 years!

Balancing Act

Each termite colony has reproductives, workers, and soldiers. They work together to survive. **Chemicals** called pheromones (FEHR-uh-mohns) help balance the colony. Termites give off and sense these chemicals.

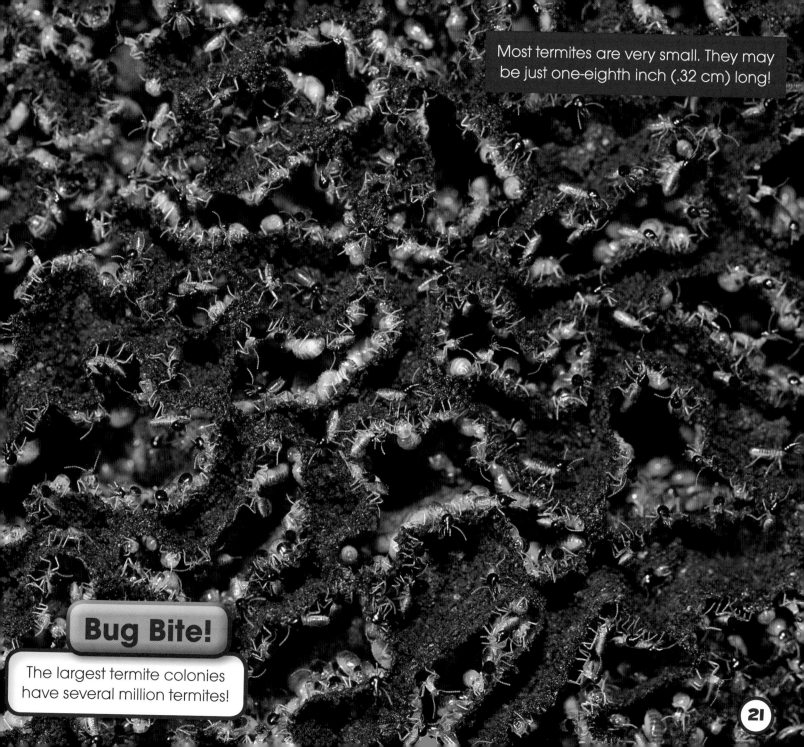

Most termites are very small. They may be just one-eighth inch (.32 cm) long!

Bug Bite!

The largest termite colonies have several million termites!

Most soldiers have strong jaws and large heads. This helps them protect their colony.

All nymphs are the same when they **hatch**. The level of pheromones in the colony causes nymphs to become workers, soldiers, or reproductives.

Workers have small bodies. They move through tunnels, cleaning the nest and caring for the young.

If a colony is out of balance, some adult termites can change jobs. To do this, their bodies molt into a new shape for their new job. This keeps the colony balanced and healthy.

Danger Zone

Termites face many predators. These include ants, aardvarks, and anteaters.

Termite soldiers **protect** their colony. Some let out special **chemicals**. The chemicals are sticky and slow down small enemies.

Bug Bite!

Some termite soldiers explode at enemy ants. They shoot out chemicals so hard, their body bursts apart!

Anteaters break into termite mounds. They smell termites and think of dinner!

Some termite soldiers use their large heads to block the tunnels in their nests. This keeps out invaders, such as ants.

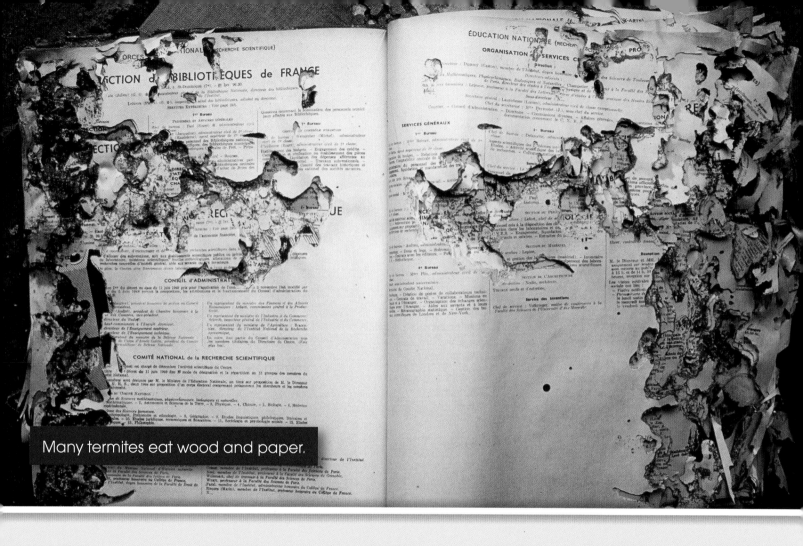

Many termites eat wood and paper.

People are another termite predator. They may poison a colony to stop termites from eating wood in their house. And in some parts of the world, people eat termites.

Termites eat tunnels into wood. This weakens and often destroys it.

Bug Bite!

About 10 percent of termite species are pests to humans.

Termites have large colonies. This is one way they **protect** themselves. Having large populations helps at least some colony members survive attacks. These members help the colony continue to grow.

Special Insects

Termites do important work in the natural world. By eating wood, they break down dead or rotting plant parts. This helps improve soil. Soil is useful for growing plants and crops. In this way, termites support life on Earth.

Termites are natural recyclers.

Bug-O-Rama

Do termites ever leave home?

Yes. Alates leave the nest. They meet in large groups called swarms. After a short time, males and females pair up to start new nests.

Did you know termites farm?

Some termites mix wood and their own waste to make a garden in their nest. They grow food there to feed the entire colony.

How big are termites?

Most termites are very small. But, termite queens may be much larger when they carry eggs. Some can reach more than four inches (10 cm) long!

Important Words

abdomen (AB-duh-muhn) the back part of an insect's body.

chemical (KEH-mih-kuhl) a substance that can cause reactions and changes.

hatch to be born from an egg.

jaws a mouthpart that allows for holding, crushing, and chewing.

mate to join as a couple in order to reproduce, or have babies.

organ a body part that does a special job. The heart and the lungs are organs.

protect (pruh-TEHKT) to guard against harm or danger.

shed to cast aside or lose as part of a natural process of life.

thorax the middle part of an insect's body.

Web Sites

To learn more about termites, visit ABDO Publishing Company online. Web sites about termites are featured on our Book Links page. These links are routinely monitored and updated to provide the most current information available.

www.abdopublishing.com

Index